Freeing Intelligence
Through Teaching

THE JOHN DEWEY SOCIETY LECTURESHIP SERIES

The John Dewey Society Lecture is delivered annually under the sponsorship of the John Dewey Society at the annual meeting of the National Society of College Teachers of Education. Arrangements for the presentation and publication of the Lecture are under the direction of the John Dewey Society Commission on Publications.

ARTHUR G. WIRTH, Brooklyn College
Chairman and Editor

Freeing Intelligence Through Teaching

A Dialectic of the Rational and the Personal

by

Gardner Murphy

Director of Research
The Menninger Foundation

Foreword by

ARTHUR G. WIRTH

Chairman, The John Dewey Society
Commission on Publications

GREENWOOD PRESS, PUBLISHERS
WESTPORT, CONNECTICUT

LB
1055
.M8
1977

Library of Congress Cataloging in Publication Data

Murphy, Gardner, 1895-
    Freeing intelligence through teaching.

    Reprint of the 1961 ed. published by Harper & Row,
New York, which was issued as no. 4 of The John Dewey
Society lectureship series.
        1. Learning, Psychology of. 2. Teaching. I. Title.
II. Series: The John Dewey Society lectureship series ;
no. 4.
[LB1055.M8 1977]   370.15'2   77-4217
ISBN 0-8371-9593-4

FREEING INTELLIGENCE THROUGH TEACHING

Originally published in 1961 by Harper & Brothers, New York

Reprinted with the permission of Harper & Row, Publishers, Inc.

Reprinted in 1977 by Greenwood Press, Inc.

Library of Congress catalog card number 77-4217

ISBN 0-8371-9593-4

Printed in the United States of America

FOREWORD

By Arthur G. Wirth, Chairman
*Commission on Publications of
The John Dewey Society*

In this fourth John Dewey Lecture a serious issue
for American education is clearly and sensitively de-
lineated. The issue revolves about differing concep-
tions of the fundamental factors involved in the processes of human learning and knowing and the act of
teaching. The choices we make will have deep significance for the quality of education available to our children in the years ahead. One approach involves a set
of assumptions leading to a highly rationalized conception of the teaching-learning process, the other is
based on a view of man's nature which assumes that
human learning and knowing involve complex inter-
actions of both rational and personal factors.

The issue itself is related to our current social situation. As a people we are confronted with a pressing
need to cultivate our total human potential, to achieve
levels of learning and knowledge that will surpass any

previous efforts in our history. The sense of urgency is compounded by our nervous recollection of the red banner on the moon and the familiar beeps signaling from the Sputniks, Luniks, and more far-reaching Russian satellites.

One part of our past impels us, when confronted with a grave national problem, to formulate the dramatic crash program approach for which we are noted. Not long ago it was fifty thousand airplanes a year that were needed to repulse the threat of Hitler; now it is education that is involved. How may the formula apply in this instance? If we conceive the problem primarily as the need to increase efficiency of production, it would be understandable if we turned readily to a sector of our experience where we have an unquestioned genius: the principles and techniques of the rationalization of work and assembly-line techniques which many times have brought forth a rich harvest. If we assume that levels of knowledge may be conceived like goals of industrial production, we might seek by analogy to discover means of efficiency for our classrooms similar to those that have worked so well in our factories. In such an effort it would be useful to picture the mind of a child as an entity subject to precise dissection, and to have a conception of subject matter as material which may be scientifically graded, organized,

6

and programmed so as to fit neatly into an accurately diagrammed mental life. If we pursue this approach with sufficient enthusiasm, we may go into action armed with scientific laws telling us how to provide proper motivation for the learning of predetermined correct responses, and implemented by teaching machines which will light up with the proper red or green signals. Our children, busy and pleasurably rewarded, will be on their way—"at their own individual paces" —as happy, efficient "learners." The school becomes a kind of *panopticon* after the vision of Jeremy Bentham, " a mill for grinding rogues honest and idle men industrious."

Admittedly this picture is overdrawn, and admittedly the alternative is not to become Luddites in education. We can learn from all carefully conceived and tested efforts to understand what is involved in learning. But before dashing headlong down this road, Dr. Murphy asks that we pause and ask if this way, so alluring in its promises, really contains a sufficient account of the human being as a seeker of learning and knowing.

As an alternative he states the bold proposition that education is, in truth, a matter of passion. No effort to free intelligence can be adequate that does not take into account the rich life of impulse, affect, and the unconscious. This is confirmed by the wealth of investigations in the biological and social sciences and in psychoanalysis. Attempts to deal with the rational in isolation from the complex of irrational components deny the true dimensions of reality about man. Before we permit ourselves to be panicked by an unseemly haste for quick answers, we might recall that we cripple ourselves whenever we shut ourselves off from reality. We know, for example, that a person's I.Q. score may be a very imperfect predictor of his eventual productivity, for a person's image of himself and his level of self-acceptance may be at least as significant as any abstract intellectual potential.

Dr. Murphy presents a panoramic overview, rich in imagery, of factors in human experience to which we shall need seriously to attend if we wish to release intelligence more fully. In rejecting overly simplified solutions, Dr. Murphy raises fruitful and penetrating questions: Does the evidence indicate that rationality can be seized by direct assault, by the "sheer encouragement of rational thought"? To what extent must the teacher who would release thinking be a student and a quickener of the impulse life? While questioning narrowly intellectualistic approaches to teaching, he does not pit systematic study and personal involvement against each other as antithetical elements.

Rather he suggests that truly effective teaching depends on understanding the complementary nature of the rational and the personal, and in seeking to bring them into fruitful relationships. The productive teaching-learning situation then becomes a transactional process in which teacher and students are joined in a reach for a more meaningful understanding of themselves and their world. While calling us to remember the key role of impulse and love, Dr. Murphy's position is not to be confused with an overly sentimental T.L.C. (Tender Loving Care) school of thought. The love that binds teacher and student is rather a shared concern for exploring the many facets of reality in which their lives are immersed.

Gradually we are presented with a conception of the teaching process that has its full share of subtle complexities. We are left as much with an art to be cultivated as a science to be applied. We become aware of many unanswered questions and the large share of mystery involved. Before the reader with a strong need for sure-fire answers turns aside in impatience, he might ask himself whether, in the long run, it may not be more satisfying to be living closer to the right questions. Teachers and students, while joined in an open-ended quest for meaning, will find themselves also sharing a genuinely humane situation.

Dr. Murphy needs no extensive introduction to the readers of this volume. In his productive career in research, writing, and teaching, he has established himself as one of America's foremost psychologists. In an era which has driven many men to gloom and despair, Dr. Murphy has retained a steady, realistic faith in man's capacity for change and self-fulfillment through processes of courageous self-discovery. Beginning his academic career at Columbia University, he later became chairman of the Department of Psychology at the City College of New York. Among the many books he has authored are his monumental *Personality: A Bio-Social Approach to Origins and Structure; In the Minds of Men,* a book growing out of a UNESCO project devoted to a study of the social tensions between the Moslem-Hindu communities in India; and *Human Potentialities,* an appraisal of emerging research results about man which aims to show "what kinds of things we shall need to know to realize our potentialities as human beings."

At present, he is director of research at The Menninger Foundation in Topeka, Kansas. Among his many duties, he is giving thought to three major projects: one is devoted to psychotherapy research; a second is concerned with a study of normal development; and the third is a project on the nature of perception in which clinical, experimental, and exploratory methods are being employed to enable us to understand factors responsible for our perception of the world and ourselves. Wherever Dr. Murphy is at work, one will find exciting adventures of the mind.

The John Dewey Lecture Series is part of the program of publications of The John Dewey Society for the Study of Education and Culture. Through this series the society aims to get before American educators and the lay public statements on various facets of the educational enterprise presented by eminent thought-provoking scholars from various sectors of American intellectual life. In addition, the society has sponsored a long list of yearbooks under the direction of Professor Archibald Anderson. Now being planned is a new series of monographs in educational theory, in which one or two authors will explore problems or ideas which contribute to the theoretical foundations of education.

The present chairman of the Commission on Publications wishes to acknowledge his gratitude for the sage advice and willing support provided by Professor H. Gordon Hullfish of Ohio State University in his capacity as President of The John Dewey Society.

JOHN DEWEY

Many of us think of John Dewey as a staunch rationalist in an era of the irrational. Others, thinking of his pragmatism and experimentalism, humanism and relativism, will remind us of the deep hostility between Dewey and the modern rationalist. Here are some issues worth struggling with, as we seek to understand modern education and the modern teacher.

G. M.

I

In the era of Immanuel Kant, for many it seemed that the capacity for rationality had forever been withdrawn. There could be no hope of knowing the things in themselves which surround us, nor any hope of knowing the nature of that inner self in which subsists the capacity for knowing. Absolute idealism did, of course, swing back into the philosophical vogue. But a traumatic doubt persisted; and when the evolutionary theory crushed the thin shell which absolute rationality had again begun to structure for itself, evolutionary doctrine plainly meant that we could know only that which finite evolving minds are equipped to know, as a part of the process of adapting to the environment. Only such intelligence as is instrumental for action can have any place in the scheme of life, and indeed we who study the scheme of life are ourselves bound by the limitations which we also find in the living things we study.

William James[1] saw this clearly and underscored

13

the evolutionary nature of the knowing mind. Bergson[2] was already heralding an age of intuition and the knowing process was itself a mere slicing device which cut cinematographic slices through the flow, the becoming, which is reality. Dewey[3]—sensing the irretrievable loss of all absolutisms and the instrumental character of thought as agency of life—saw the issues at the philosophical level as he used such terms as "experimental logic," and at the same time at the homespun level of kitchen, dairy, and playground as he penned his examples of *How We Think*. Through all these same years Sigmund Freud (as deeply imbued with evolutionism as were James and Dewey, but more romantic and poetic in his conception of the upward spiral of evolving life) found the instinctual, the irrational, as prior to the capacity for ordered thought. Yet, as the ego evolved, he gave it a place of greater and greater power. "Where Id was, there shall Ego be."[4] "The voice of the intellect is a soft one but it does not rest until it has gained a hearing."[5] Paradoxically, Freud was thus the most ardent rationalist of the three; rationalist, at least in the sense that he believed that a formal contact with a reality outside of us is possible. Yet he, too, found the rational arising from the irrational.

Taking to heart such matters as I listen to modern theorists of education, I cannot help but be intrigued; disturbed, yes, but enlightened and challenged, too, by the revival of educational research in pure rationality. This is not just an American vogue. In the Soviet Union, for example, we have seen the attempt to introduce the rational and ordered structure of the Russian language into the elementary school curriculum years before the formal training in declensions, conjugations, genders, and idioms had been attacked. It has become the aim of the Soviet educator to make everything as rational and as conscious as it can be made. In the current systematic analyses here in our own country, the effort is being made to lay bare the structure of intellectual operations in the child so that the subject matters will fit hand in glove the logical structure of the child's mind. The intriguing new investigations by Piaget[6] into the relations between logic and psychology have been capturing many bastions in which, day before yesterday, the immaturity, the confusion, the irrationalism of childhood had been accentuated. Poor old Kant! So great is our need for order—a need to which I shall try to give attention a little later—that we are bound to find it pursued, as we read in *The Hunting of the Snark*, pursued "with forks and hope" until all the meat is taken off and only the clean glistening wishbone, the pure homuncular thought that Faust found encased in a bottle, can manifest its capacity to lay bare the real which is outside of us, the real that is inside of us, and the process that connects the two. The rational has come riding back from the era of Kant and of Darwin on the wings of modern science and mathematics.

Now is this not a little bizarre? Have not the scientists told us with soul-searching earnestness that they encounter no absolute reality? As with the pot of gold at the end of the rainbow, they who have vainly pursued it have been the first to tell us that it is not there. Have not the mathematicians reminded us that they only play an eternal game with things imagined according to rules which have been contrived to be followed for the intrinsic gratification of following such rules, and with no possibility that this eternal dance could enable us to grasp the solid substance of reality? Mathematics, they say, gives contact with reality and makes predictions possible only because of gross stuff out there which is unknowable, though it be processed somehow by assumptions leading back again to empirical, irrational sense-perceptions which belong in the same mute, unknowable world as the original observations.

This enigmatical universe, for example, contains invisible stars known to exist not by virtue of being seen but by virtue of perturbations exerted on the movements of other bodies which can be seen. Indeed the invisible companion of Sirius can be weighed as well as visible stars nearby. One can start out with odd, irrational, empirical observations such as the curvature of light. Connect these with other irrational, intrinsically meaningless observations dealing with masses and movements; put all this through the miraculous transformation of a mathematical system which deals with things that cannot exist, such as square roots of negative numbers, and come back again into the world of prediction, stating that energy in measured form will arise from certain chain reactions, and we come out with the exquisitely simple $E = MC^2$.

Now this, of course, does not prove that the universe itself is irrational—far from it. It seems to indicate, however, that in the name of the *rational* a great theoretical task can be done which is itself not capable of a fully rational definition. As Dewey himself remarked, there is indeed a world in which logical process follows unerringly from a cycle of rational operations, but the espousal of such a system is to forego the potentiality of talking about the real world. The Einsteinian operations just described can indeed be carried out and can bring us back again through the tortuous devices of the mathematician into the real world again; in fact, the frighteningly real world which we wish very much we could somehow avoid, the world of energies which are both incomprehensible and uncontrollable. The fact remains, however, that the empirical observations are simply marks, "pointer readings," made on sense organs and processed by an intricate machinery of evolutionarily given processes in nerve cells. And they bespeak, as James pointed out, the specific structure of the evolved nervous system in which they inhere, giving us not a mind which transcends biology but a mind growing out of the selective and adaptive functions which we know as evolution, and intelligible only in reference to the relations of certain organisms to their habitats. We cannot even set the limits on the areas to which adaptation may prove feasible. Bridgman has even reminded us that the absolute laws which characterize the present cosmos as far as we know it may have a drift of their own and no longer fit other types of equally real universes.

None of this is to decry rationalism. Many of the rationalists, in decrying the pragmatist note which James and Dewey have sounded, seem to act as if all these cautionary tales were nihilistic rejections of thought and of order. Perhaps the logicians betray in this way a certain unwillingness to let the implications of evolutionary thought sink in.

Now if this were just a philosopher's quarrel, I would do well to stay out of it. But when I hear some investigators speak as if the thought processes which their studies laid bare were the actual thought processes employed by real children in relation to real tasks, I cannot but assume that the track has been jumped. For just as the child is struggling to make a sound abstraction from empirical fragments, which are themselves irrational, so the educator is trying to find in the total activity of the child a cleanly separable, discernible, isolable thought process, which exists and can indeed be measured as an attribute of the age and the endowment of the individual child. An abstraction which is valuable, as any Jamesian or Deweyian system would agree! But it has—it seems to me—been reified; the child, at the moment that he is confronted with rigidly grade-placed materials, is treated as a child who is cleanly—as it were, surgically—deprived of his impulsive and motivational life; indeed, a child capable of being dealt with in the manner of $E = MC^2$. There is an empirical question whether the child's mind can be operationally treated, or I might say almost literally operated on, with a sharp, clean scalpel like this, so that actually the subject matters in the school can be definitively ordered with reference to the logical progress from one type of logic to another.

This is an empirical question. I have hinted my reasons for skepticism, but I must not do more. I must not insist that this will not work. I must only ask that we be given massive and systematic empirical evidence, carefully sifted, replicated, and tested for statistical significance—processed, if you like, with high-speed computers and shown to apply to a cultural mass of which the child is a component part; in other words, that it be given the whole modern "works" before it be solemnly written down as a new star in the educational firmament, which we should see in the East and with our camels pursue until the little one has actually been found there waiting to start on his pure rational trajectory, successfully orbited through life. It will be a free, clean, strong mind, because we have chosen to clean it up, sterilize it, and set it free on these terms!

But even while standing in awe of such powerful tools, a little doubt may remain. The problem of the

20

learning mind—the problem of the mind of the learning child or adult—is an empirical problem, and no theoretical doubts can be taken too seriously in a world bristling with such complexities as ours, until it can be shown that this is in fact what the freeing of the intelligence of the child consists of.

II

There are, in the meantime, some other possibilities as to the ways in which intelligence may be freed. It may be worthwhile to remind ourselves that even before the era of Darwin, James, and Freud, thoughtful men had asked persistently whether rationality may not be the child of irrationality, and indeed have wondered whether it might not be the last-born child of primeval chaos and the void. Much of the early philosophy of Greece had accented the irrational, the Dionysian; Lucretius had drawn rationality and order from the fortuitous concourse of atoms. Indeed, with Plato himself the creative force is love, and in the Fourth Gospel the Logos, the Word, of the opening chapter is soon replaced by the all-encompassing love which is identified with the Deity. In the Darwinian system there can be simian and ultimately human rationality, because the nervous system has blindly moved out beyond the blind impulse to meet the raw threat of annihilation. Never denying the reality and the immense survival value of rationality, the Darwinian system grafted rationality upon instinct, as Freud was to do later. These thoughts suggest the parallel that the nurture of rationality may perhaps lie in other efforts than the sheer encouragement of rational thought; indeed, that the rational may best continue to grow in the instinctive soil in which it was engendered, and that too clear and sterile a surgical separation of thought from its ancestral and parental roots in love and impulse may threaten its viability. And if this should by any chance be true, it would mean that the learner must not be deprived of the riches of his impulse-life, and that the *teacher must be a quickener of that impulse-life through which thought can grow, indeed a shaper and molder of impulse into the rationality which comes from a healthy craving for contact with reality.*

But just how can love give birth to rational thought? Let us try Freud first. The conception that understanding is bred of love was expressed in the psychoanalysis of fifty years ago in terms of a pervasive biological creativity, from which images, symbols, and

22

relationships could be invested as if they were persons. There could be cathexis upon the person, his face, his form, his voice; so, too, cathexis upon one's own person as represented in the story of Narcissus. From this it was not too far-flung an effort of the imagination to conceive of cathexis upon the acts, physical and mental, carried out daily with others or with oneself, so that one could love not only the mother, the mother's voice, the tone of her voice, but tone in general, or that melodic line or abstract Grecian contour of beauty which contains the internal essence, the abstract form of music. One might go on to say that if there is love to begin with, love can reach out and entwine within itself all of the things, acts, and relationships of this world. It can even come to love the very process by which it differentiates, analyzes, and makes meaningful reality out of this turbulent world. It can become a love of the structure and order of the world, like Spinoza's intellectual love of God; or it can, as in Nietzsche's imagery, love both the order and beauty of Apollo and the frenzied dance of Dionysus. It can love the act of knowing and the act of thinking. It can give rise to, or coalesce with, the act of comprehending. From this point of view the great task of education is to evoke an understanding love, to fan its flame, to make creative love broader and deeper, reaching for all that exists, as in the spirit of Walt Whitman, to whom the poetic fire was given to write, "poetry belongs to real things and to real things only."

Everything that is real comes soon to be invested with an active, seeking love. Many a little child loves the shaft of the sunbeams through the nursery, the dew on the grass, the salty splash of the sea, and loses this as he grows up into the world of rationality. As Wordsworth said, "A sordid boon." But with the love of a mother, or the love of a teacher, not only the brightness of the dew on the grass, but the sparkle of the mind itself can resist such a "drying up." The seeking intellect craves all that is, and the teacher is one who can hold up realities to be seen by the pupil and can convey, by all the means we have described, the sense of the real, instilling a passion for that which has the "demand quality" of real things and of real things only. The teacher helps the child to discover for himself a reality which is then shared; rather, realities which the child bumps into, hears, smells, fingers, looks at, manipulates, enjoys. For the child the excitement of such contact—instead of stifling thought—can become its beloved foster parent and guide it to the real. The child makes abstractions on the basis of his own direct, often unique experience.

This does not mean that the teacher's personal enthusiasms are the sole basis for the ordering of the rich substance of life. Insofar as the teacher discovers order, coherence in the things and ideas presented by the world, his passion for the real applies to the order discovered as well as to the separate objects, events, and ideas. The teacher loves order and conveys this to the child. But the pupil is seeking order, too, hand in hand with the teacher, and indeed often discovers order more clearly, more personally, because it arises out of his own experience.

Education is a matter of passion because passion is the mother of understanding. Can I seriously mean this? Is not the teacher charged with more than the responsibility to convey enthusiasm, or even more than the understanding begotten by enthusiasm? Is it not the task of the teacher to teach the capacity to discriminate? In other words—going beyond the love of the real and of the order which expresses the real— is it not the teacher's responsibility to engender a willingness to face and to judge all of reality, whether noble, threatening, irrational, or trivial? Is not the freeing of intelligence both a matter of freeing *for* contact with the significant and freeing *from* the frightening or the debasing? Does the teacher not only need to free the inquiring mind of its fears, but to free it from the fetters which go with all the pettiness and triviality of a timid and cautious world? Can we by any stretch of the imagination equate two teachers, one of whom instills a passion for collecting bits of information and the other who collects a few central, profoundly pivotal realities regarding the structure of the cosmos or of human life? Is there not in the very concept of intellectual freedom more than the concept of indiscriminate voyaging over a boundless sea of new experience, experience without quality or value, but defined solely in terms of its magnitude, its diversity, or its newness? How can unbridled enthusiasm be equated with education? We are, indeed, all familiar with the "scattered student," who responds to everything, sparks the class, bubbles with insights, but never finishes or comes through with a careful piece of work, never gets the deep satisfaction of accomplishment.[7]

Yes, the teacher must help to give focus. But I am not sure, in the case of an inspiring teacher, that the issue has not been drawn in terms of an unreal contrast. Is there necessarily an intrinsic conflict between encouraging the spontaneous curiosity, interest, enthusiasm, and love of knowing in the child, and also guiding him, helping him to focus, organize, master thoroughly and proudly the skills and insights involved in the areas of his most eager knowing?

I believe that such questions will yield their own answer. I believe we shall discover that there is for the inquiring mind a hierarchy of significance, with a place for all reality, but a place in an ordered system. Perhaps the mind which gluts itself indiscriminately upon thousands of facts is itself a mind which loves reality but little. There is an intrinsic sense, or order and system, in the world of meaning, which—just because the world itself is ordered and the human intellect likewise ordered—can lead from one love of reality to a still more comprehensive love of reality. The role of the teacher will not be fulfilled by turning over a thousand stones, but by enabling the child or youth to see in the stone which arouses his interest the history of this world, the evolution of its waters, atmospheres, soils, and rocks, prying into deeper meanings "just because they are there." I believe this makes a great difference to the teacher's conception of the process of learning and the process of teaching.

III

I shall never forget the day I had the privilege of taking William Heard Kilpatrick out to see Moreno's demonstration of psychodrama[8] at Hudson. Adolescent girls, mostly somewhat retarded intellectually, who had gotten into trouble with the law, were being given a normal schooling with vocational training and a rich social life by Fanny French Morse, and Moreno had come there to set free the personality potentials of the girls through free enactment of little scenes into which they could project themselves. We had learned beforehand only that the psychodrama gave each participating individual an opportunity to throw herself immediately and without preparation into any social role that had meaning for her. Twenty-five girls were waiting for us. "Now girls," Moreno said, "it's a hot afternoon in the summer. You, Pauline and Helen, are driving along the parkway and pull up to a roadhouse. You, Ruth, are Helen's little daughter. You, Hazel and Janet, are the waitresses. Mary, you are the proprietor. All right, go ahead, girls." However remote this situation might be for urban lower-class girls, they threw themselves into this scene with imagination and energy. It was a great show. Then Moreno would say, "All right, you girls there, criticize this play." Eunice, Viola, and Grace had comments immediately. "Helen didn't act like she was really hot and tired; anybody could see Hazel wasn't really waiting on tables; she got nervous; she talked too fast." These girls were learning social membership by enacting it, and this was a part of a vivid scheme of social education now being given a somewhat psychiatric coloration. There was no doubt whatever that the girls were learning in the sense in which John Dewey used the term.

On the way back in the car, Kilpatrick made a remark, suddenly pulling a world of uncertainty into a knot and posing a dilemma with clarity. "If Moreno," he said, "is as much as half right, Thorndike is more than half wrong." He paused. I could not think of anything worthy to reply to such a remark. "If Moreno is as much as half right, Thorndike is more than half wrong!" This was patently John Dewey speaking through the lips of Kilpatrick in an inspired utterance. That Sunday in 1935, when both Dewey and Thorndike were still alive, epitomized the problem of the law of effect, or what we today would call reinforcement learning. Wait until you get what you want, then *reward* it. If something you don't want happens, *ignore* it, or in certain situations, *punish* it. But many of these girls had already been punished by life over and over again, and had gone on doing the punished thing. Moreno had hit upon the fact that social motivation and social reinforcement are often inseparable; or rather, if you know the motivation, you do not have to apply—cannot apply—external rewards and punishments. Moreover, if you know motivation, if you know where life is going, you know that reinforcement, when effective, consists of allowing the motivation to pursue itself, as indeed all modern educators from Pestalozzi onwards have seen. There remains a place—but how limited a place—for the external reward-punishment treatment!

There is, however, another package rolled into Kilpatrick's statement. Moreno held in this case the teacher's role. When he has failed, as he sometimes has, I think it has been due to the authoritarianism of the teacher's role. When he succeeded, as he often has brilliantly (as in that day at Hudson), it came from the simple, natural, direct, fatherly handling of co-workers and co-learners in a situation which all could share. Note the ease with which the assignments were made, and especially the atmosphere in which the girls could criticize the work of their peers in a casual, matter-of-fact way. Note the way in which the Moreno program fitted into Fanny French Morse's emancipation program as a whole.

John Dewey, it is you to whom we are chiefly obligated for this vision of active and democratic education in the public schools, the instilling of socially significant habits derived from the common needs of ordinary people! It was not even merely the fulfillment of the child's motivations; it was the fulfillment of the child's need for contact with her peers; the fulfillment of her need for parental support, warmth, and direction; the fulfillment of that discipline which lay in the task itself rather than in external authority; the fulfillment of a role a little harder than she was ready for, so as to constitute a challenge, a forward push into the domain of life that lay ahead. To supply this was the role of the teacher.

IV

We also believe now that there is an instinctual craving for the world of understanding; the child is barely three when he bombards us with questions probing into realities he is newly discovering. He

31

craves to discover, to think, and to find that things make sense. Love of the structured rational order is one of the main bridges between Dewey and psychoanalysis, and though often neglected, is such a major component in our mode of traveling between the great modern systems of the mind that I shall take the liberty of developing it at length. The thought with which we begin is that the instinctual life is not necessarily rooted in the vital organs but springs just as much from the cells of the central nervous system, indeed from all the cells of the living body; that the organism is a craving kind of thing and that it craves commerce with the reality which engulfs it. I shall spend a few minutes on the modern problems of psychoanalytic ego psychology, in which this thought has been developed.[9]

The idea is simple. The primordial psychic reality for the individual is not impulse alone, but is both impulse and cognition. The organism is equipped with devices for making eager contact with reality, and not only such indirect contact as arises from conflict and conflict resolution. There is, in other words, an innate capacity for effective reality seeking and testing, exactly as a rationalist would seem to demand. Suppose, however, that these forms of hunger for reality become strong in the higher mammals and become overwhelming in man, proliferate until they become a massive controlling force. Suppose that what the fully developed human being wants is the world in all its fulness, to understand it and to interact with it. Here I should like to share with you some thoughts developed in a conversation with Nevitt Sanford, of the University of California. The ideas as I shall state them are primarily his, secondarily mine; they arose "transactionally" as each responded to the other.

If we believe that there are huge, rather formless masses of energy in the newborn, not yet poured into narrow and specific channels, and if we believe that there are similarly primitive ego activities of searching, scanning, and enjoying the world, which we may call ego drives, we can grant that the former groups of activities may enrich the latter without ever saying that the latter derive *all* their force from the former. This could be put into the older psychoanalytic language by saying that the ego energies are derived from the id energies; but I should prefer to state this in such a way as to give a prominent place for "conflict-free ego spheres" of primitive delight in sensory and motor activity, and in the many forms of reality contact. Later appear at a more structured level many forms of contact with one's own "insides" and the building of a self-other system of relations. The apparently impassable gulf between Dewey's "rationality" and Freud's "irrationality" may be well bridged by conceiving of needs as initiating activity, but needs as themselves extending far beyond the matrix of visceral or organic tensions. We may follow James and Dewey in believing that nothing happens without motivation and that the thought processes are themselves motivated, organically fulfilling. We may be more optimistic than Freud with regard to the kind of rationality achievable, but we shall remember Freud's dictum that the voice of the ego is persistent. While granting with Freud that there is a vast realm of unconscious life of which we are scarcely aware, and a world of which Dewey was relatively ignorant, we may still agree that Dewey, in company with James and the Darwinian evolutionists, saw that the mainsprings of action lie largely in a deep-seated, persistent need for cognitive orientation to life.

These ideas, developed in interaction with Nevitt Sanford, with whom I have evidently shared a parallelism of thought, brought to mind an image as we talked: the image of a huge mushroom-like shape, in which vast quantities of energy push up from an unknown and uncharted subterranean energy source, and when they reach a certain elevation begin to spread out sideways, forming a huge dome, as in the analogy of an atomic energy release. Sanford, talking of Vassar students, stressed the fact that the student, having once found joy and competence in the use of her mind, may rapidly reach out horizontally or vertically, or at various kinds of angles between, to master more and more subject matters in terms of a conflict-free dynamic. Unconscious conflicts may still be there, but they are irrelevant. They are bound or, perhaps one might say, rendered unimportant by the sheer masses of higher level energy now appearing in the expansion of this nuclear cloud. The process of repression is not necessarily a piece-by-piece inhibition of low-level activities. Rather, there is a massive and structured ego activity which can take in stride the momentary threats occurring at one or another point below the surface and can move sidewise and up, enriching and structuring the world of joyful and sustaining ego activities. The world of interpersonal relations and of the transmission of culture may thus be conceived not only in terms of the structuring of id energies, but in terms of transmission of the torch from one free ego to another.

35

The intensely precious intellectual and aesthetic world of an educated adult is the confluence, or integration, of elements which come from sensory hungers—like the hunger for tone, color, rhythm, and the deployment of spiraling patterns in time and space—but it is also the confluence and integration of higher-order structuring tendencies that arise in the life of concepts and of symbols. There is a place for raspberry sherbet and for Beethoven's Ninth Symphony; for a splash of sunset color and for a Rembrandt portrait study of an old man. And every experience contains primitive sensory and visceral components and higher-order constructs; all of these, if the man enjoyed his education, resonate to the rhythm of his earliest experiences with mother and father, playmates, and teachers. There is empathy, identification, transference, in every phase and. at every level.

From this viewpoint, the teacher is carrying out no sleight of hand, no manipulation of displacements and sublimations, when he or she enriches, strengthens, catalyzes, and gives new directions to the life of thought. This is modern psychoanalytic ego psychology. The irrational processes found in early cell division in the prenatal period can, as the fetus achieves a richer central nervous system, become the anatomical and physiological basis for the activation of a rich rational existence. This conception that rationality is a built-in need and not just a mask for the irrational is one which the educator would do well to use. He need not depend on secondary rewards or rely mainly upon substitutions. He may trust the guided and developed mind of the young seeker in terms of his own sensory hungers, cognitive hungers, craving for reality contact. The fact that the teacher wishes to share understanding can enhance the process, but both he and the pupil turn their love and understanding not only towards one another but towards the rich, real world to which both give their allegiance. Love is central but "love is not enough."[10] This kind of rationality comes right out of the evolutionary process, like Dewey's instrumentalism, and need have no commerce with either the older or the newer types of absolutism.

This conception that the pre-rational love of *outer reality* can guide us into reality contacts would apply to all our sensory hungers, our reality needs with reference to the surrounding world of stimulation and challenge. There is, moreover, within us a world of *inner* stimulation and challenge, an *inner* world of physiological response, of memories, of images, and of fantasies about which we have always known, but about which we know vastly more today as a result of the labors of physiology and psychoanalysis. It is a world in which we become aware of the role of scanning and searching for organic and kinesthetic sensations, a world rich in its discriminable experiences, a world of inner sensation compounded richly with memory residues and with high-order conceptual formulations, the delight of the phenomenologist and the existentialist, and for that matter, the poet and the prophet. The rationalist of today, with his earnest curiosity, need not be troubled by the thought that egoistic, or for that matter narcissistic, components may play their part in his interest in his own internal doings. The inner world has become just as real as the outer world; hardly anyone in an odd corner dares any more to refer to the world of fantasy as "unreal." It may be called a different kind of reality, but even this does not seem coercive or constraining upon us. Man, as man, has been liberated by the processes of detached concern with the very organism itself as he knows it, to a point where rationality can be one of the most exciting phenomena in the world. James's concern with the "Stream of Thought" seems today a rather mild and timid approximation to the riches being discovered as physiology, experimental psychology, anthropology, and psychoanalysis, probe the reality-testing functions as these are found in the sensory and memoric, fantastic, and cognitive realities within us.

The teacher who responds to this inner world can convey it, just as he or she can respond to the outer world, and in the spirit of the Dewey-Bentley transactionalism[11] may respond to the two-way traffic across this bridge, setting free day by day some of the remaining remnants of the organic and instinctual life which have not been brought into relation to the outer challenge, and setting free the seeking and scanning functions which have timidly clung to the so-called outer world and have not caught the vision of considering as well their brethren of the world within. In the cell assembly doctrines of Hebb,[12] the curiosity and love investigations of Harlow,[13] the Rapaport[14] materials on the functions which protect us for creativeness as we stand between inner and outer, and the Bykov[15] conception of interoceptive and proprioceptive conditioning which ties us to the exteroceptive world, the learning mind may turn in upon itself and watch the process of learning which leads into thinking. As Lawrence Kubie[16] has pointed out, the world of creativeness depends upon freeing oneself from the over-coercive constraints of the merciless pounding stimulation by the outer environment and also of the concordant throbbing impulsive world of within, as we stand on the threshold between the two.

This has much within its substance that restates the older classical association psychology, the Apollonian-Dionysian constructs of Nietzsche, the conception of the subliminal self as developed by Frederic W. H. Myers,[17] and the modern ethologist's concern with the "demand quality" which makes all the difference between a raw cold sensation and a demanding or commanding sense perception reality to which the organism is drawn. We can gratefully use here McDougall's conception[18] that there is an inborn and integrated response at the same time involving cognitive, affective, and conative terms. We may regard the little graylag gosling of Lorenz, which so intently follows its mother or any other moving object, as finding an irresistible demand quality which leads into the looking, listening, and following, from which follows the act of pursuing this overwhelming stimulus.

It is this demand quality of the rational to which Soviet psychologists of today give primary attention;

the process, as Elkonin puts it, of making everything as conscious as possible. Yarmolenko suggests that the urge to understand is just as fundamental as the urge to eat. The classical answer to the question of the relation of the rational to the irrational lay with the distinction between the associationist principle and the principle of motivation. It was long the psychologists' effort to show that these two forms of reality were utterly distinct. On the contrary, it has been our effort here to show that if not in fact identical, these two forms of motivation—the impulse to know and the impulse to gratify the inner needs—are two aspects of one reality. The cognitive need is as commanding and constraining, and at the same time as fulfilling, as any realization of the more primitive organic needs.

I do not believe that the full force of this restatement of the relation of instinctual needs to the process of thinking has been grasped, despite the fact that experimental psychology, physiology, cultural anthropology, and psychoanalysis have all been pointing the way. Indeed, I think that Dewey failed to grasp all of this, partly because he was born too soon to see the full flowering of psychoanalysis, partly because he feared the irrational. Dewey's insistence upon the dignity of rationality compares oddly with the romantic fashion in which James and Bergson contrasted the irrational with the rational, and their tendency to give the irrational a special place in cosmic structure and in human life. James suggested, as he introduced us to *Pragmatism,* that we all lie on inclined planes. Let him who lies on an *un*tilted plane cast the first stone. Here the parallel between James and Freud is striking, while Dewey passes down the other side of the road. Through all this it is curious to find Dewey's insistence on making everything as rational and as conscious as possible, just as we have quoted the Soviet psychologists as doing. I cannot help feeling that the Calvinist Vermont here in the Dewey of the mid-nineteenth century is not completely outgrown even in the transactionalist Dewey of the last years. It is odd to find these residues of an older theory of thought. The Dewey and Bentley[19] transactionalism is at home when it recognizes cognitive hungers which go out to meet the demand quality of the outer world, and could indeed be as well made to turn to the inner world if the subject matter of psychology, and particularly of psychoanalysis, were to be more adequately stressed.

Does all this mean that the teacher simply responds to all which simply stirs response in the child? I think not. It means, rather, that the interpersonal relations of teacher and pupil, and the pupil's potential response to the reality waiting to be discovered, are two aspects of one learning process. The irrational and the rational are intimately blended in the teacher's communications, as they are in the intercommunications between the members of the group which is learning. The clarifying merges into the electrifying. Indeed the clarifying, just by being clarifying, can become electrifying. Much would depend upon the subject matter. There are different ways of teaching different subject matters, different forms of electrification on the part of teacher and on the part of the taught.

V

But part of the irrationality lies in the unresolved irrationality resulting from our incomplete knowledge of the psychology of individual differences; differences among teachers and among pupils. Dewey's concern with individuality saved him from an over-refined rationality. There is a huge need for empirical studies of different kinds of teachers who communicate, inspire and set free different potentialities. Abstractions of the sort appearing in the Conant[20] report are not so much false as misleading, because the individuality of the learning process tends in this way to be blurred. Our strange ignorance of the psychology of the teaching situation after all these decades of research on education involves an ignorance of the individuality of the learner, which even the Sarah Lawrence studies[21] have not dispelled. There are still great roadblocks to the development of sound theory of communication in the teaching process. Psychoanalytic and psycho-social views of the communication process, as seen by Follett,[22] Lewin,[23] and Moreno, have only charted a sea in which we are told communication will be productive; they have not yet told us of the individual islands and archipelagoes which make communication feasible in this vast sea. The liberation of individual potentialities remains largely a hope and a dream, while the networks of communication between the various individual islands are as yet blurred, and our first vague studies of group dynamics are so lacking in a clear communication theory relating to mutual liberation of unconscious dynamic components.

VI

Suppose we should set up a half dozen practical rules for the teacher guided by these modern principles. Suppose we should say that intrinsic rather than extrinsic satisfactions must be used by the teacher: that the teacher must remove sources of fear and suspicion and evoke a glow of cognitive satisfaction; that he must allow or encourage identification between the pupil and the teacher insofar as he wishes to share the delight which he feels in the subject matter or the process of learning. Suppose that he knows how to convey the love of the subject matter and of the very process of intellectual discovery itself; suppose that he should make much of the curiosity components in the things to be learned and emphasize progressive mastery of subject matter. All of this we could confidently share with the teacher in the sphere of progressive education. We could not, however, tell him what to do with the child who at a particular time craves not only intrinsic but also extrinsic motivation, who wants both physical and social rewards; the child who cannot identify with the teacher but seeks identification in other persons or even in the men of other eras. Suppose that we should decide in certain cases that not the simple freeing of a latent potential but the deeper resolution of conflict will be necessary. We shall need to develop, in other words, an applied science, almost an engineering science, related to the teaching process. We know that this already exists in rudimentary form, and as we talk to good teachers we constantly hear of examples. The psychology of interpersonal relations, however, is still in its infancy and as you will see if you look at almost any textbook of group dynamics or of leadership in industry, community life, or education, the sage but abstract rules unduly dominate those little human concrete particulars which would make the difference between intelligent guesswork and genuine competence in suiting the message to the individual child. It is the psychology of individuality itself and of interpersonal relations, which—as Dewey brought out in his books and papers on social psychology—is a necessary corrective to the more abstract principles about democracy and education.

The individualistic Dewey from Vermont founded the Chicago laboratory school in 1896, and wrote *Democracy and Education*[24] twenty years later. It was the school's privilege to go down the democratic road past the conception of uniformity of subject matters and the shared knowledges and skills which all members of a democratic community need to encompass, and to consider the schoolhouse as a center within which as many different individual minds emerged as there were individual children. Those who began to protest against progressive education as giving undue liberty or even as lacking in discipline, and even those who, with the Hundred Best Books slogans, insisted that the men and women of a democratic community must share the same fundamental intellectual content, still saw that it would be a mortal blow to all education if standardization of mental operations actually became a goal. The Dewey of *How We Think* was a democrat in a Jeffersonian sense, one who believed in the variability of human beings, by virtue of which a tent big enough for all such individuality, permitting freedom of movement of all such individuality, must be devised. The role of the teacher in relation to human intellectual emancipation is one which emphasizes the biological individuality which evolutionary theory has emphasized. The teacher must help the learner to believe in his own individuality and his capacity to learn.

VII

I have reflected here on some interrelations between the intellectual edifices erected by James, Freud, and Dewey. It would be easier to select a single hero. Our hero-worshipping need is to feel that some one person conceived and communicated the great master key to the communication process which we call education. The need is great to conceive of a dominant individual—like Darwin in the field of evolutionary theory, Einstein in relativity theory, Freud with reference to the theory of the unconscious—as catching the central reality and lifting it from its murky hiding place for all to see with one vast sweep of the genius's mind. Like Carlyle, we want to make history the story of the lives of great men. I feel this temptation strongly. I believe, however, that our understanding of the nature of the rational and the irrational in the discovery of the ways of this world, and of our own deeper nature, has been a slow and difficult achievement in which the gnarled roots of many systems of thought are intertwined in fantastic complexity. I believe that the conception to which we are moving would owe a great deal to the forms of inquiry associated with the names of James, Dewey, Wertheimer,[25] Freud, Piaget, and many more. But Dewey himself, with his early conception of the sociology of knowledge, was one of the first to realize the sociocultural nature of thought, and the fact that it is ultimately society, not the individual, that realizes the potentialities in any given way of thinking and feeling, discovering and creating.

He who concerns himself with this process of creation encounters in the complexities of modern genetics the fact of such rich potentialities as no man can today define, and such rich possibilities of interaction with his comrades as to force the judgment that the possibilities for a creative teacher are literally boundless. I do not mean to suggest that there are no biological laws, and no laws of interpersonal relations that can establish solid guidelines for the cultivation of teaching skills. I mean rather that skills proliferate into the kind of regions suggested by skill in the violin, skill with the painter's brush, skill in embroidery, skill with rod and reel, skill in the management of men. These tasks do indeed require training, but far more they involve a perpetual stretching of the imagination to try to see a little way ahead at all times into newly emerging potentials in the mind of child and youth.

Perhaps this is one reason for the relative failure of most of our modern excited research studies into creativity since the Sputnik excitement caused us to emphasize creativeness. Perhaps there is no single psychology of creativeness. Perhaps the classical formulations, valuable though they may be, yield essentially single formulations selected out of a virtual infinitude of possibilities of creative process. Perhaps there is literally no more a psychology of creativeness than there is a psychology of music, or a psychology of science. Perhaps all the ranges and reaches of psychology can be explored up and down without even beginning to tell us what the varieties of creative thought may be. If this is true, the attempt to teach teachers to teach creatively may require a caution against proceeding crabwise from one activity to another, side by side with it in complexity and importance, rather than moving into greater depths or ascending to greater altitudes. It could be that we are climbing a mountain; it could even be that we are rising from our little launching pad of today into regions which we are yet unable to define.

I believe that these issues are colored and shaped in large measure by considerations of the personality of the individual teacher in relation to that of the individual child or youth. I am not commenting merely upon the various attempts to standardize methods of selecting teachers, and the teaching of teaching skills in a rather gauche attempt towards interchangeable parts in an industrial society with corresponding levels of supposed competence, experience, and effectiveness. Most of us see through this, and the danger is temporary. I refer rather to a considerably deeper and less easily soluble problem: the fact of identification of the child with the teacher in the process of learning. Identification means selective openness, the readiness to incorporate the teacher within the personality of the learner, and with this the conscious and unconscious assumption of attitudes and values, often quite far reaching, which—as it were—pre-commit the learner not only to certain outlooks on subject matter but life as a whole.

With the ancient Guru of India, there was the deep commitment to the view that for years upon end the youth would incorporate within himself the basic attitude of the teacher. This way of thinking in our own society, in a relatively unpretentious form, seems to have lain behind the conception of continuity of teachers during the grades, and even in the junior high school and the high school, in the thought that such continuity is strength for the learner even though the progressive specialization of modern subject matters may mean less and less explicit competence of the individual teacher in the newly essayed, specialized subject matters. When it comes to general science, or a general view of social science or literature, it is agreed that it is not so scandalous to let one teacher handle the diversities and complexities. Let the physics, however, be really physics, and not just part of a general science course, and we are scandalized if the biologist tries to teach it; this seems to involve a lack of respect for the subject matter, even for the learner himself.

The issue to which I draw attention is the likelihood that with increasing specialization in his own studies, the child will require more and more identification models; there will be a model in his mind regarding a physics teacher, a French teacher, a history teacher; and his choice of vocation may be "built in" as a consequence of the choice of models and the way in which the models interact with the specific subject matters. The child must fit his own incompletely formed personality into these various models or molds as well as he can. Some of his pre-professional difficulties, I believe, are connected with this phenomenon.

I am not sure that the problem is soluble without more facts. I would stress, however, two equally serious dangers: one, that education become fragmented for the individual in terms of the proper approach to take when you see life in terms of experimental science, the proper approach to take when you see life in terms of the historian, or as the specialist in literature. These fragmented or specialized viewpoints not only prevent the spirit of science from entering into the study of history and the spirit of appreciation of the beauty of this world from entering into the study of science, but convey a feeling of the impossibility of communication between the various cells in the chambered nautilus which make up the partitioned mind of the learner. It follows that such creativeness as he achieves is creativeness within subject matter, not creativeness with reference to life, not creativeness with respect to new modes of integration which lie there in the structure of the world.

Despite the efforts at interdisciplinary collaboration we have not found the way out, and I wonder if we do not need a good deal of research on the possibilities of establishing what we might call generalists, as well as specialists, in our advanced teaching as well as in our orientation courses; whether we might not develop and emphasize a type of college or graduate educational material consisting not simply of "great books" from the past, but the more profound integrations of today. We might indeed, as has been suggested, turn the curriculum upside down, and after progressive specialization in high school and the early college years we might give the last two years of college to the cultivation of an educated man's or woman's realization of a point of view expressive of the modern realities as we know them, and of the individuality of the unformed learner himself. The kind of creativeness which might arise from such a process might be a true interdisciplinary creativeness. It might not only counteract the post-Sputnik urge to finer and finer specialization, but might—at least for some of us— attempt the kind of integration which can only be attempted when genuine competence in various specialized subject matters has already proceeded quite far.

VIII

Now as to the opposite danger: the danger of over-personalizing the process of education. The individualistic quality of the present approach might perhaps suggest that the role of a teacher in sharing his love of subject matter or method is to bring the pupil, with a sweeping gesture, into the orbit of his own basic interests; to make the pupil emotionally like himself. Now there is a certain amount of truth in this, as there is in the statement that the process of identification depends to a considerable degree upon love, and that unless there is some kind of love for the teacher a new subject matter is likely to have hard going. There lurks, however, a danger in this formulation. It may be pushed to the point of implying that an irrational adherence to one view of life must exclude other views; that the teacher as partisan in the world of ideas must make loyal disciples; that there is in point of fact no real emancipation except into that larger intellectual bailiwick over which the teacher presides. The whole conception of the evolving mind, however, as these experimental and clinical studies have suggested, is one in which there is literally no predetermined position to which the learner must arrive, whether it be his teacher's position or any other. There is genuine creativity in a deep sense.

There is, as a matter of fact, the release of potentials which go much deeper than our present study of genetics or of the social sciences would have predicted. We seem to be discovering in the pupil's response to music, for example, something far beyond adherence to the teacher's school of thought or feeling; some deep responses to the rhythmical structure of the world as wave theory defines it. We seem to have realities which are both biological and trans-biological. It is not a substance that the mind is seeking but rather a form of action. There are in fact many forms of action, many response rhythms, far more than we dare today to guess. It is the responsibility of the teacher to set free a certain sort of capacity for resonance, for varying sensitive resonance. The mind is a potential mover in all directions, not, of course, unbiased or equally predisposed in all directions, for that would not be in the nature of organic structure, but with a readiness dependent upon rich structural possibilities.

It is not the teacher's responsibility to set going in the pupil simply the resonance which the teacher himself exhibits, as when you hold down a piano wire and sing to it to elicit from the wire that particular imposed rhythm which your own voice at that time demands. On the contrary, we must somehow conceive the liberation, through eager inquiry, of this sort of seeking for resonance, until the resonance is found which at the moment brings a phase of reality into intimate relation, into a sort of meshing relationship, with the outreaching mind of the learner. There is, indeed, a little of the irrational here in the sense at least that there is no compelling logic by which a given starting point must be followed step by step through a logical chain to a particular predetermined final result. There is, however, a system of real steps toward the discovery of such realities, and a series of processes of emancipation by which the learner using the resonances of the teacher makes contact with forms of resonant-making reality to which he had previously been opaque.

It is one more case of love, the irrational, setting free the child whom we call reason. The teacher who can embody and implement such a relationship can teach more than subject matters, can teach more than skills, can teach a certain readiness for life. A teacher who knows the individual richness of the resonance patterns of mankind will not try to mold a pupil into his or her own image—he will know, deep in his bones, that the pupil must be himself. A school system in a democracy which knows the never-ending resources of both physical and social reality to meet the needs of the mind, will never demand a forced or fixed pabulum to be fed to all. Indeed, it will never make the mistake of assuming a fixed relation between learner and what is learned. "The spirit bloweth where it listeth." This may call for a good deal of what Santayana called "animal faith" or perhaps it may just call for a lot of love of human beings, their diversity, their unfulfilled quality, and the unfulfilled quality of the society in which incompleteness of individuals requires the realization of deep, unknown potentials, forms of fulfilling interrelationship which may develop between them.

What I have said is offered as a minor contribution to the problem: Can a teacher teach rationality in such massive unreason as flourishes in our time, and the panic which often halts the efforts to re-think our twentieth-century predicaments? We have often set up a false antithesis between the personal and the reasonable. We have sought, in depersonalized rationality, a mode of making genuine contact with an impersonal reality outside of ourselves. We seem to believe not only that the teaching of scientific subject matters can make men and women who share the scientific spirit, but also that somehow an age of science-mindedness, an age of rationality, might supervene. There remains, however, a possibility of storming the fortress of the irrational by less frontal assaults, by more reasoned circuitous routes. It may be that a study of the personal interrelations between teacher and taught—of those who are taught in school, college, and advanced study, in fact—may yield far more regarding the cultivation of deep thoughtfulness.

I shall try to put the issue simply by stating the question:

> Can the teacher teach rationality? My answer will be "yes," under five conditions, which assume that there is: (1) freedom from demoralizing fear; that rationality is not an object of terror for the learner; that the ego strength is adequate to accept and to use constructively the normal range of daily anxieties and challenges; (2) a love of the subject matter and of the system of knowledge and skill and world order of which it is a part; there must be cathexis upon subject matter, the process of confronting it, and the meanings which emerge from mastery of it; (3) cathexis, too, upon the very methods themselves, by which such rationality is sought; a love of learning in Spinoza's sense; (4) underneath such a process, acceptance of one's own self,

cathexis upon the self as seeker, knower, lover of reality; and finally, (5) in every relation between teacher and taught a full transactionalism, the teacher being taught, the student teaching, the two learning and teaching in reciprocity.

We must stress individual differences, both qualitative and quantitative, in all of these processes. In reality, paradoxically, we would admit that a young man or woman, deeply imbued with love of some of the realities which today's science and scholarship yield, might seek it out despite the obdurate hostility or blind pedantry of an unwilling teacher. In the long run, however, we should say that the hope of the individual to find a world on which his mind can feed, depends on these sympathetic interpersonal processes. By the same token, the hope of mankind to discover meaning in the universe and a way of living together in brotherhood, must depend not only upon the inventiveness of statesmen who seek new modes of world order, and not only upon the eternal plea for brotherly love, but upon the integration of these two modes of seeking reality; a personal love both of the learners and of what they learn, the cultivation of a groping need for one another and for ideas; as Lawrence Frank[26] would say, a tactile immersion in the persons, things, and events in this world to which rational models are indeed a profound help, but never offer the living substance.

These ideas are as old as Plato. But in each age they are negated or ignored as one seeks fresh abstractions, and our own age of scientific abstractions with its dissection of the learning process, the thinking process, into clear rational components, has apparently already shaken some of the confidence and blurred some of the vision of the great tradition in the teaching art. We need, therefore, to keep coming back in a swinging spiral to the same arc of the circle through which we had earlier swung, but now with a mounting region of perspective, a broader outlook. At our peril we may, if we like, construct an educational process by selecting students who appear to be superior on certain tests, by selecting teachers who meet certain supposedly objective criteria, by arranging funnels of interchange between teacher and taught which involve frictionless and painless modes of ideal reciprocity from one to the other, placing this whole body upon a chassis of a world ordered by the very incarnation of rationality itself. If, however, the human organism is not so constructed as to allow its central nervous system to operate independently of its autonomic system, its glands of internal secretion, and its sensory and motor equipment, if such rationality as it has depends upon biological functions with an evolutionary past and an instrumental adaptive present, would it not be more likely that the teacher would teach well if he accepted the full biology both of the pupil and of himself? And would he not—in a society composed of individuals—do a more constructive job if he conceived education transactionally as a bio-social process, in which rationality is bio-socially defined and the real, instead of being placed solely at the door of the rational, is seen as the creature of the life process itself?

FOOTNOTES

[1] James, W. *The Principles of Psychology,* 2 vols. (New York: Holt, 1890).

[2] Bergson, H. *Creative Evolution* (New York: Holt, 1911).

[3] Dewey, J. *How We Think* (new ed.) (Boston: Heath, 1933).

[4] Freud, S. *New Introductory Lectures on Psycho-Analysis* (New York: Norton, 1933).

[5] Freud, S. *The Future of an Illusion* (London: Hogarth, 1928).

[6] Piaget, J. *Logic and Psychology* (New York: Basic Books, 1957).

[7] Murphy, L. B., and Ladd, H. *Emotional Factors in Learning* (New York: Columbia, 1944).

[8] Moreno, J. L. *Psychodrama* (New York: Beacon House, 1959).

[9] Hartmann, H. *The Ego and the Problem of Adaptation* (New York: Int. Univs., 1958). Also see Rapaport, D. (14).

[10] Bettelheim, B. *Love Is Not Enough* (Glencoe, Ill.: Free Press, 1950).

[11] Dewey, J., and Bentley, A. F. *Knowing and the Known* (Boston: Beacon, 1949).

[12] Hebb, D. O. *The Organization of Behavior* (New York: Wiley, 1949).

63

[13] Harlow, H. F. "Motivational Forces Underlying Learning," *Learning Theory, Personality Theory, and Clinical Research,* The Kentucky Symposium (New York: Wiley, 1954).

[14] Rapaport, D. "The Theory of Ego Autonomy: A Generalization," *Bulletin of the Menninger Clinic,* 1958, 22:13-35.

[15] Bykov, K. M., and Gantt, W. H. *The Cerebral Cortex and the Internal Organs* (New York: Chemical Publishing Co., 1957).

[16] Kubie, L. *Neurotic Distortion of the Creative Process.* (Lawrence: U. of Kansas, 1958).

[17] Myers, F. W. H. *Human Personality and its Survival of Bodily Death,* 2 vols. (New York: Longmans, 1903).

[18] McDougall, W. *An Introduction to Social Psychology* (Boston: Luce, 1908).

[19] See Dewey and Bentley.[11]

[20] Conant, J. B. *Revolutionary Transformation of the American High School* (Cambridge: Harvard, 1959).

[21] See Murphy and Ladd.[7]

[22] Follett, M. *Creative Experience* (New York: Longmans, 1930).

[23] Lewin, K. *A Dynamic Theory of Personality* (New York: McGraw, 1935).

[24] Dewey, J. *Democracy and Education* (New York: Macmillan, 1916).

[25] Wertheimer, M. *Productive Thinking* (New York: Harper, 1959).

[26] Frank, L. K. "Tactile Communication," *Genet. Psychol. Monogr.,* 1957, 56:209-255.